FAURÉ, G.

THEME AND VARIATIONS

Opus 73

FOR THE PIANO

No. 817

INTERNATIONAL MUSIC COMPANY

511 FIFTH AVENUE   NEW YORK CITY

PRINTED IN U.S.A.

A Mademoiselle THERESE ROGER

THEME AND VARIATIONS

Quasi Adagio (♩=50)

GABRIEL FAURE, Op. 73
(1845-1924)

Published by International Music Company, New York City

Lo stesso tempo ($\quarter = 50$)

pp

1.

dolce e sostenuto

A

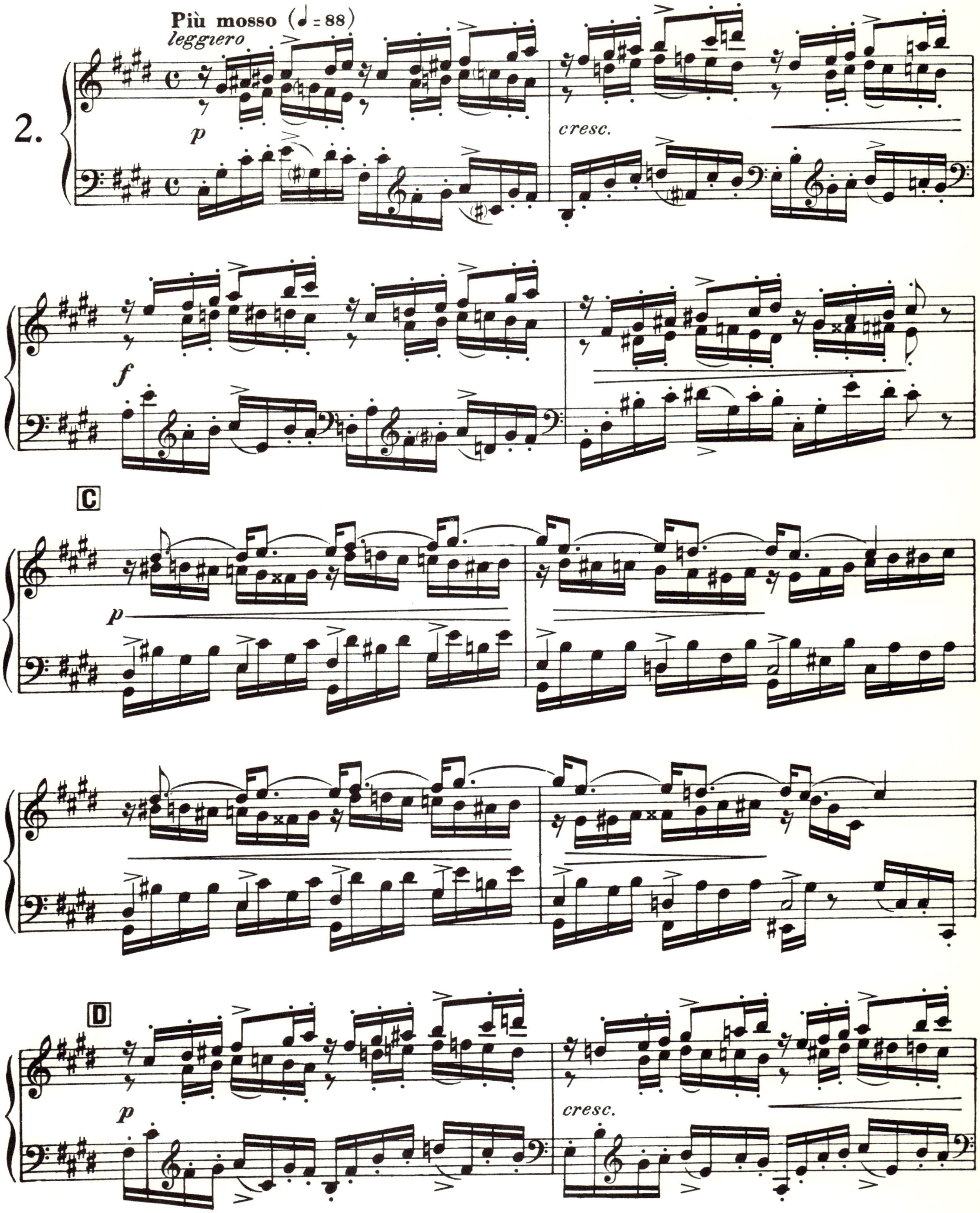
Più mosso (♩ = 88)
leggiero
2.
p
cresc.
f
C
p
D
p
cresc.

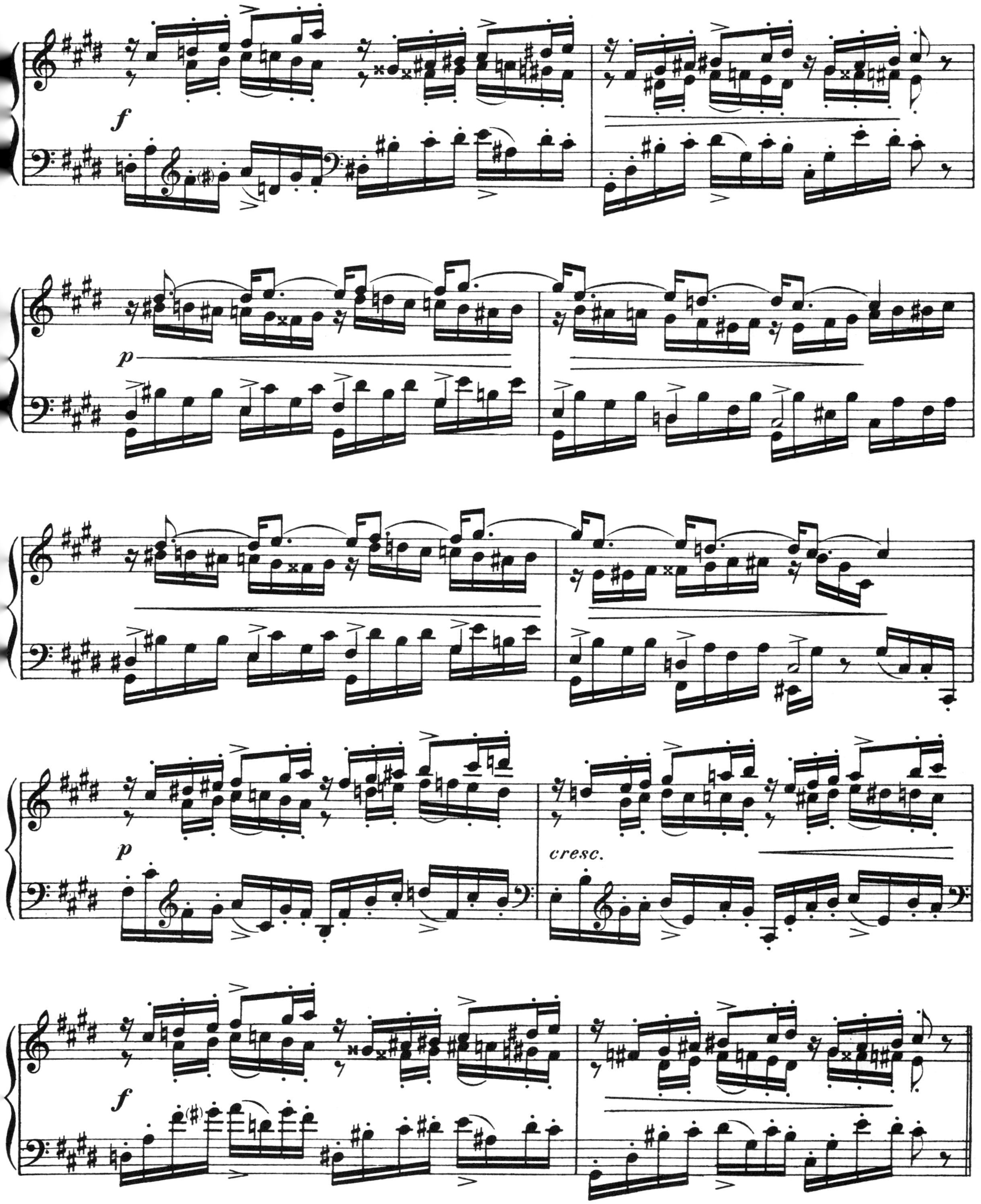
f
p
p
cresc.
f

Un poco più mosso (♩= 104)
3.
mf
marcato
cresc.
f
sf
sempre f
dimin.
E
p espressivo

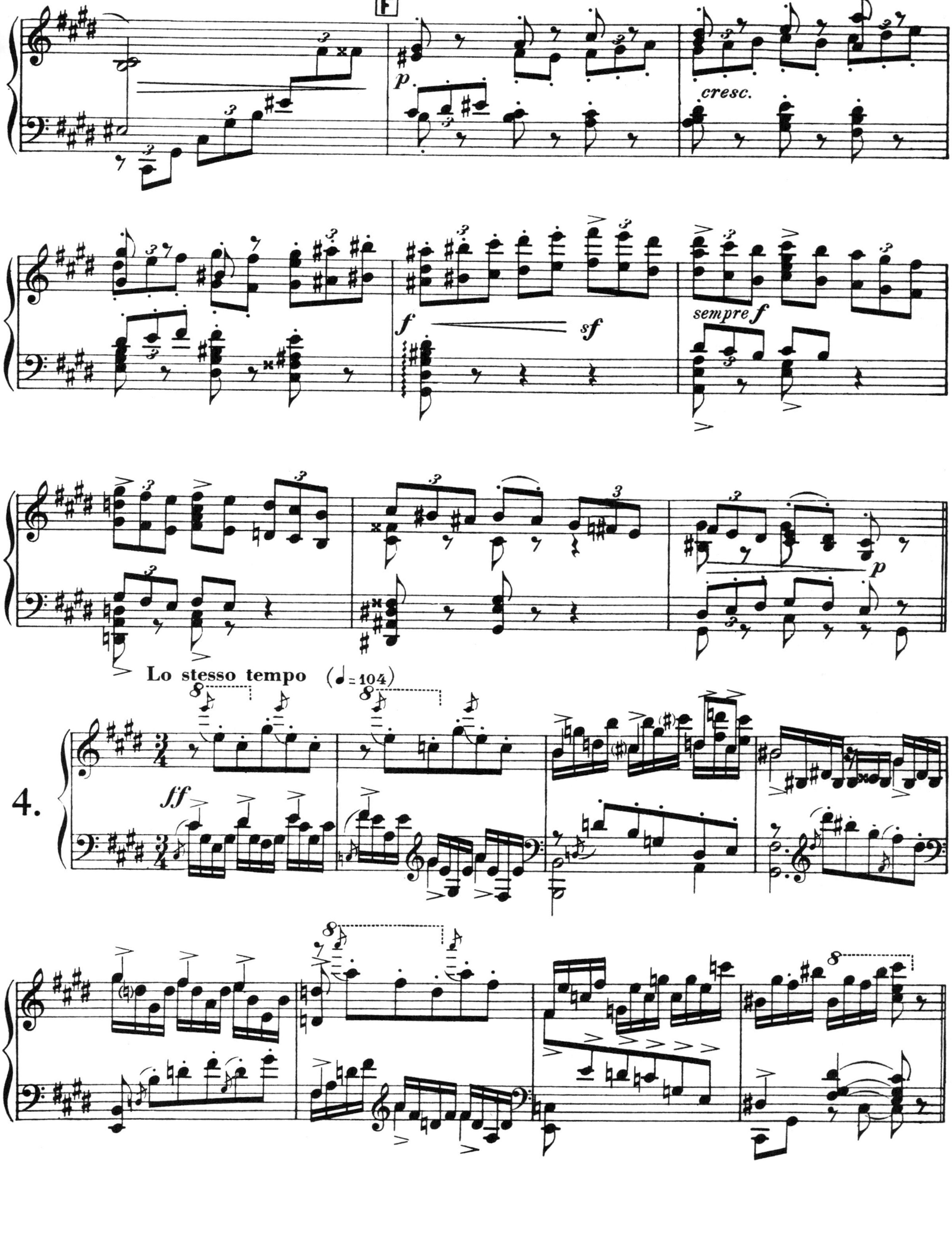
F
p
cresc.
f
sf
sempre f
p
Lo stesso tempo (♩= 104)
4.
ff

8

5.
Un poco più mosso (♩=116)
p
cresc.
8
f
sempre f
dimin.
I espress.
p
cresc.
f
p
cresc.
f
rit.

Molto Adagio (♩ = 40)

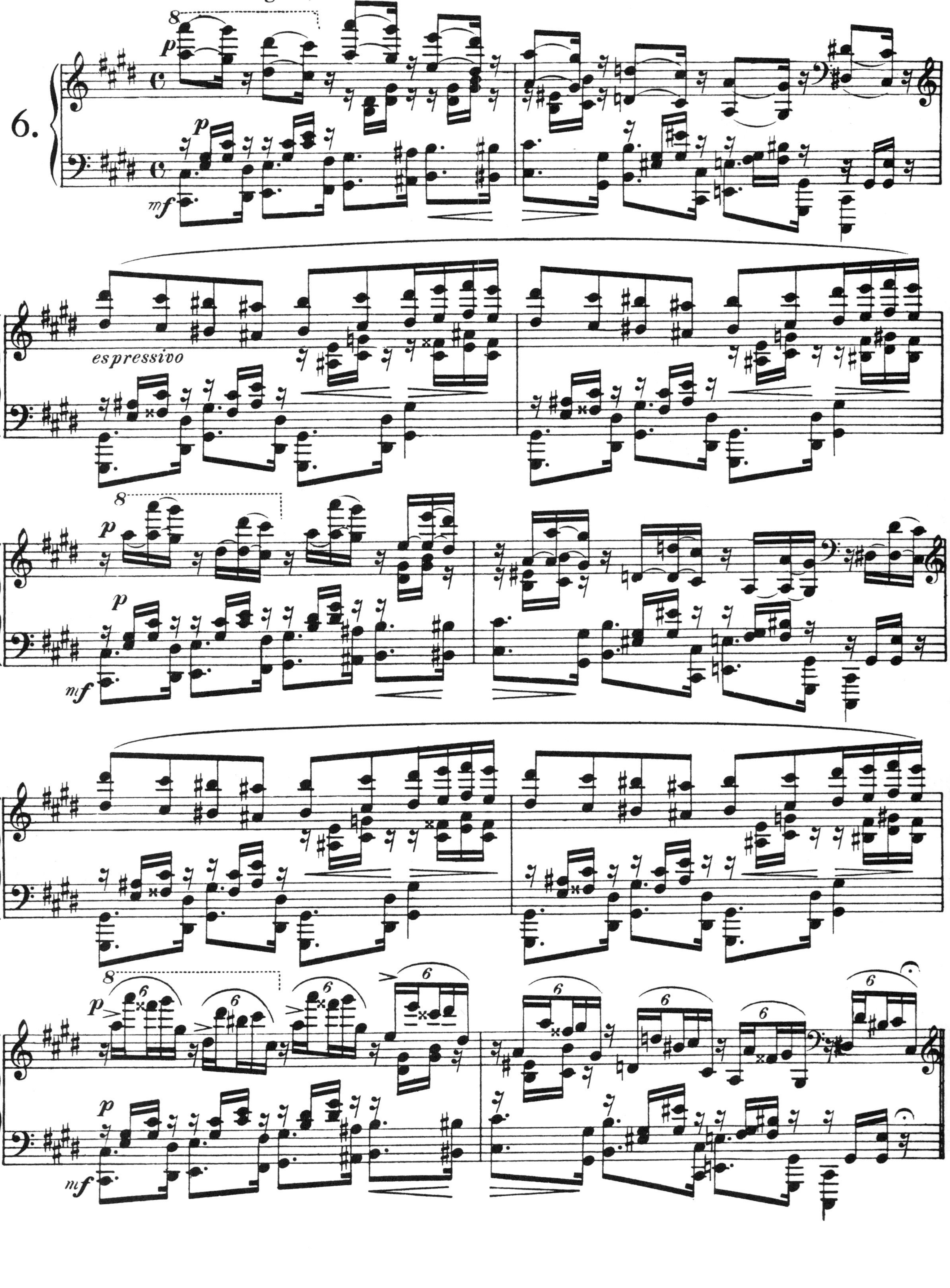

11

7.

Allegretto moderato (♩=69)

p legato espressivo

cresc.

J *espressivo*

p

f

cresc.

f poco rit.

8.

Andante molto moderato ($\quarter = 56$)

p

un poco marcato

sempre p

9.

Quasi adagio ($\quarter = 48$)

dolce

dolcissimo

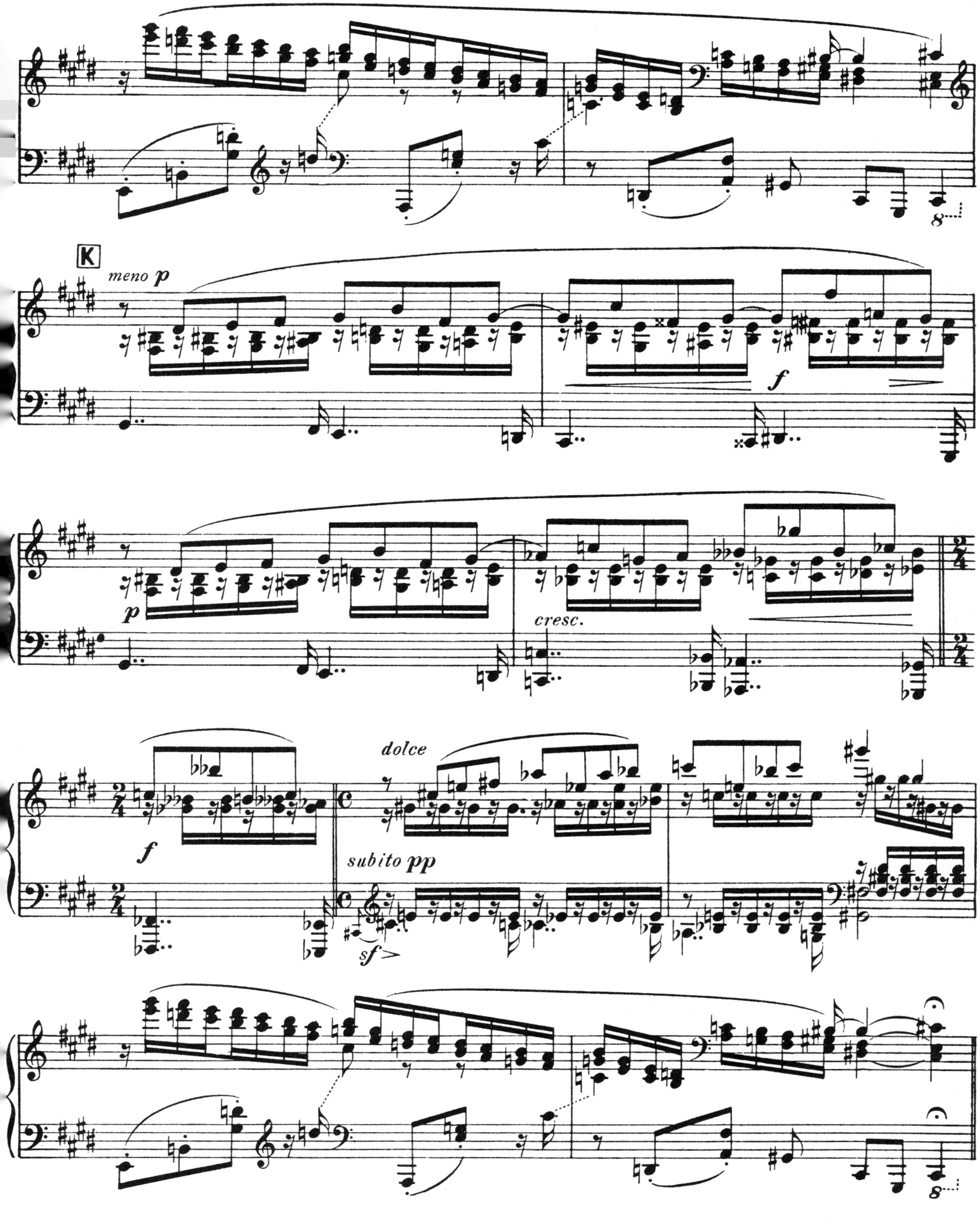
K
meno p
f
p
cresc.
dolce
subito pp
sf
8

10. Allegro vivo (♩.=104)

15

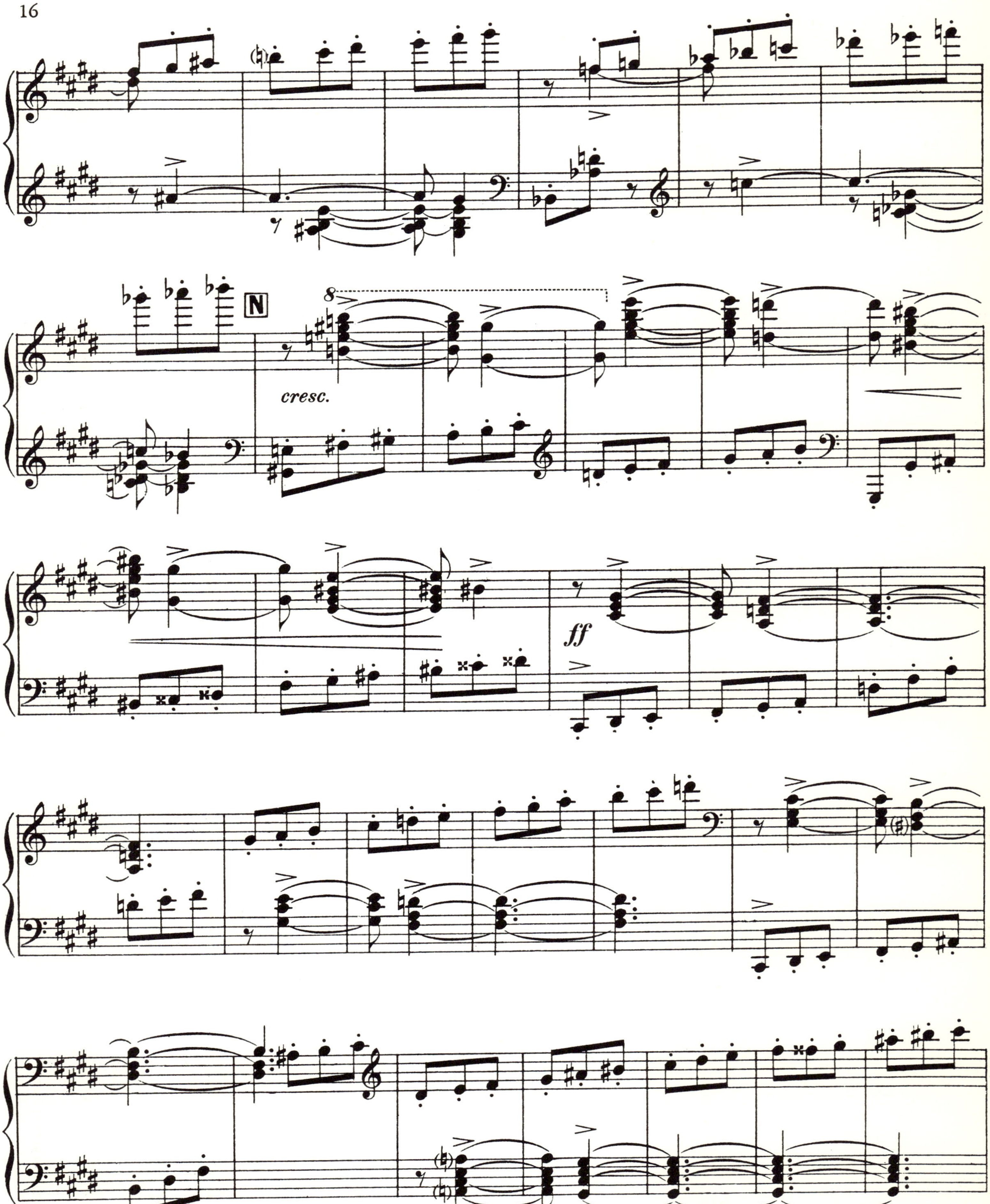
N
8
cresc.
ff

17

Andante molto moderato espressivo (♩ = 56)

11.

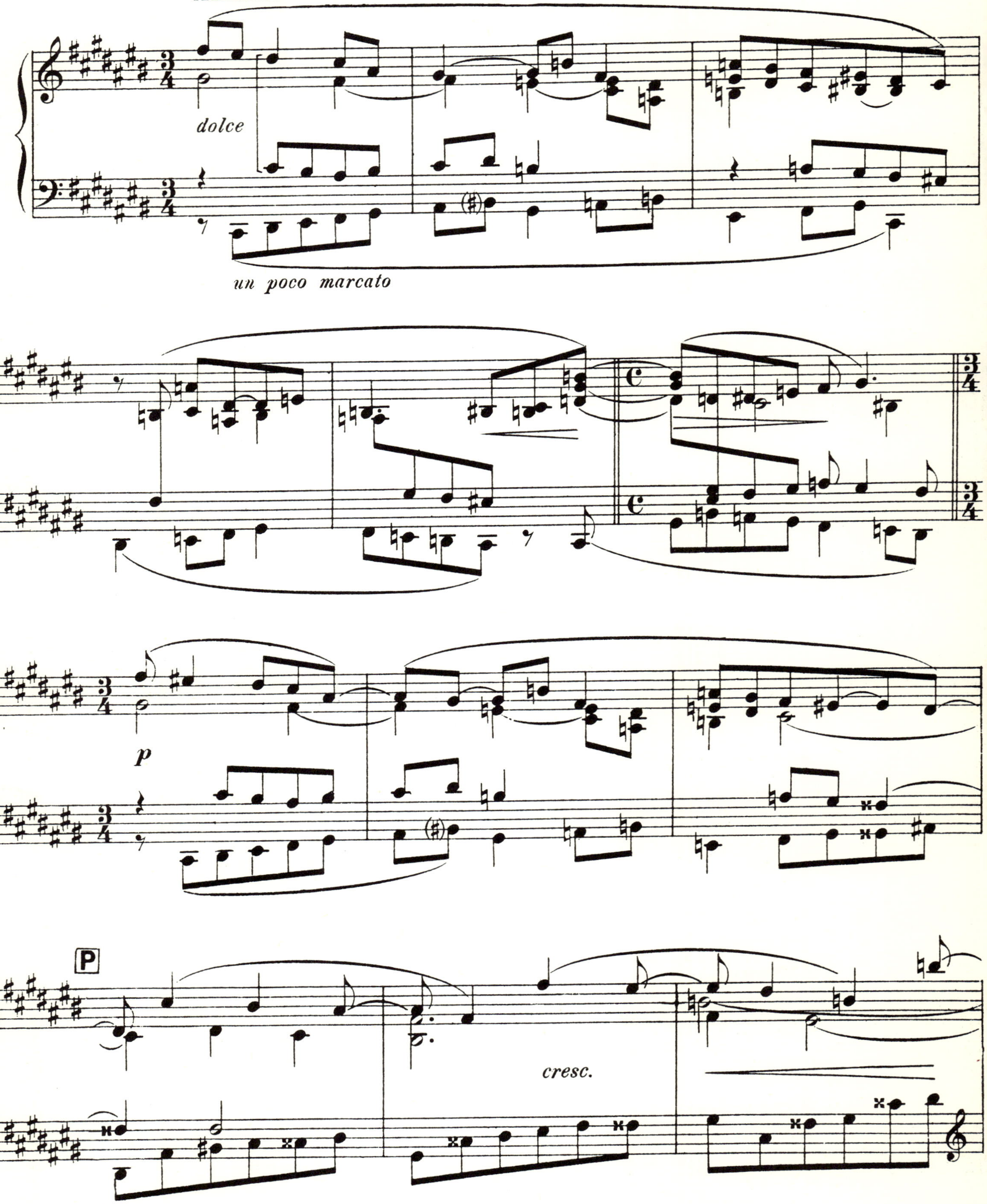

19

PIANO MUSIC

PIANO SOLO

ALBENIZ, Issac
Iberia. Suite. Vols. I, II, III, IV. Each 2.50
  I. 1. Evocation; 2. El Puerto; 3. Fête Dieu à Seville
  II. 1. Rondeña; 2. Almeria; 3. Triana
  III. 1. El Albaicin; 2. El Polo; 3. Lavapies
  IV. 1. Malaga; 2. Jerez. 3. Eritaña
Suite Española. Complete *(PHILIPP)* 2.50
  CONTENTS: 1. GRANADA *(Serenata)*; 2. CATALUNA *(Curranda)*; 3. SEVILLA *(Sevillanas)*; 4. CADIZ *(Saeta)*; 5. ASTURIAS *(Leyenda)*; 6. ARAGON *(Fantasia)*; 7. CASTILLA *(Seguidillas)*; 8. CUBA *(Nocturno)*.
Op. 165. España *(Six Album Leaves)* 2.00
  CONTENTS: 1. Prelude; 2. Tango; 3. Malagueña; 4. Serenata; 5. Capricho Catalan; 6. Zortzico.
Op. 232. Cantos de España *(Airs of Spain)* 2.00
  CONTENTS: 1. Prelude; 2. Orientale; 3. Under a Palm Tree *(Spanish Dance)*; 4. Cordoba; 5. Seguidillas.
Recuerdos de Viaje *(Travel Impressions)* 2.50
  CONTENTS: 1. En el Mar; 2. Leyenda; 3. Alborada; 4. En la Alhambra; 5. Puerta de Tierra *(Bolero)*; 6. Rumores de la Caleta *(Malagueñas)*; 7. En la Playa.
Rumores de la Caleta *(Malagueñas)* 1.00
Navarra 1.50
Leyenda *(Asturias)* 1.00

BACH, Carl Philipp Emanuel
Six Sonatas *(BUELOW)* 3.50
24 Pieces *(VRIESLANDER)* 1.75

BACH, Johann Sebastian
Italian Concerto *(BISCHOFF)* 1.50
Partita No. 1 in B♭ major *(BISCHOFF)* 1.50
Chromatic Fantasy & Fugue *(BOGHEN)* 1.50
Concerto in F min fir Piano & Orchestra.
  Two-piano score *(EDWIN FISCHER)* 2.00
Concerto in G min for Piano & Orchestra.
  2-Piano score *(GOEDICKE–PHILIPP)* 2.00
The Little Music Book of Anna Magdalena.
  12 selected pieces *(PHILIPP)* 1.25
Organ Prelude and Fugue in E flat major
  (St. Anne's Fugue) *(BUSONI)* 2.00
  1.25

BACH, W.F. — VIVALDI
Organ Concerto in D minor *(STRADAL)* 2.00

BARTOK, Béla
16 Pieces for Children *(PHILIPP)* 1.50
Sonatina *(PHILIPP)* 1.25

BEETHOVEN, Ludwig van
Op. 77. Fantasy in G minor 1.00
Op. 89. Polonaise in C major 1.00
Op. 119. Bagatelles. 11 Pieces 1.00
Op. 126. Bagatelles. Six Pieces 1.00

BORODIN, Alexander
Scherzo in A flat major 1.50

BRAHMS, Johannes
Complete Piano Works *in authentic edition.*
  (Urtext). Volumes I, II, & III. Each 5.00
NOTE: This is a *complete* edition of BRAHMS' Piano Works.
VOLUME 1: 3 Sonatas, Op. 1, 2 & 5; Op. 9. Variations on a theme by Schumann; Op. 21, No. 1. Variations on an Original Theme; Op. 21, No. 2. Variations on a Hungarian Song; Op. 24. Variations and Fugue on a theme by Handel; Op. 35. Variations on a theme by Paganini.
VOLUME II: Op. 4. Scherzo; Op. 10. Ballads; Op. 39. Waltzes; Op. 39. Waltzes *(Simplified edition)*; Op. 76. 8 Piano Pieces; Op. 79. 2 Rhapsodies; Op. 116. Fantasias; Op. 117. 3 Intermezzi; Op. 118. 6 Piano Pieces; Op. 119. 4 Piano Pieces.
VOLUME III: Study after Chopin; Rondo *(Perpetuum Mobile)* after Weber; Presto after Bach (Versions I & II). Chaconne after Bach *(for the left hand)*, Theme and Variations; 10 Hungarian Dances; Cadenza to J.S. Bach's Concerto in D min; Cadenzas to Mozart's Concertos No. 17 in G maj, K.453; No. 20 in D min, K.466 and No. 24 in C min, K.491; Cadenzas to Beethoven's Concertos No. 3 in C min and No. 4 in G maj; 51 Exercises.

BRAHMS, Johannes (cont'd)
Selected Piano Works in authentic edition:
51 Exercises 2.00
Op. 15. Concerto No. 1 in D minor.
  Two-Piano score 3.75
Op. 83. Concerto No. 2 in B flat major.
  Two-Piano score 3.75
Op. 35. 28 Variations in A minor on a theme by Paganini. Complete 2.00
Op. 39. Waltzes 1.25
Op. 76. 8 Pieces *(Capricci & Intermezzi)* 1.50
Op. 118. Six Pieces *(4 Intermezzi, Ballade & Romance)* 1.50
Op. 119. Four Pieces *(3 Intermezzi and Rhapsody)* 1.50

CASADESUS, Robert
Cadenzas to MOZART'S Concerto No. 22 in E flat major (K. 482) 1.00

BUXTEHUDE, Dietrich
Organ Prelude and Fugue in D minor.
  Transcribed by SERGEI PROKOFIEFF 1.00

CHABRIER, Emmanuel
Pièces Pittoresques
  10 Pieces *(BEVERIDGE WEBSTER)* 2.50
  1. Paysage; 2. Mélancolie; 3. Tourbillon; 4. Sous Bois; 5. Mauresque; 6. Idylle; 7. Danse Villageoise; 8. Improvisation; 9. Menuet pompeux; 10. Scherzo-Valse.
Habanera *(PHILIPP)* 1.00
Idyll *(PHILIPP)* 1.00

CHOPIN, Frederick
Nocturne in C sharp minor (Op. Posth.) .75
One of the most beautiful of Chopin's Nocturnes, recently discovered, and not included in any collections of Nocturnes.

CZERNY, Carl
Op. 33. Variations "La Ricordanza" 1.50
One of VLADIMIR HOROWITZ' favorites and recorded by him.

DEBUSSY, Claude
Suite Bergamasque *(PHILIPP)* 1.75
Claire de Lune *(PHILIPP)* 1.00
Estampes *(Suite of 3 Pieces) (PHILIPP)* 2.00
Soirée dans Grenade *(from "Estampes")* 1.00
Jardins sous la pluie *(from Estampes")* 1.00
Images. Set I *(PHILIPP)* 2.00
Reflets dans l'eau *(from "Images")* .75
L'Isle Joyeuse 1.25
Pour le Piano. Suite *(PHILIPP)* 1.75
Prelude from "Pour le Piano" *(PHILIPP)* 1.00
Petite Suite. Complete *(PICCIOLI)* 2.00
  1. En bateau; 2. Cortège; 3. Menuet; 4. Ballet.
En Bateau *(PICCIOLI)* .75
2 Arabesques. Complete *(PHILIPP)* 1.25
Arabesque No. 1 *(PHILIPP)* .75
Arabesque No. 2 *(PHILIPP)* .75

FAURE, Gabriel
8 Nocturnes. Complete *(PHILIPP)* 3.75
Op. 17. Songs Without Words 1.75
Six Barcarolles. Complete 3.00
Three Impromptus (Op.25, 31. 34) 2.00
Op. 36. Nocturne No. 4 in E flat major 1.00
Op. 37. Nocturne No. 5 in B flat major 1.00
Op. 73. Theme and Variations 1.75
Op. 84. 8 Pièces Brèves 2.50

FRANCK, César
Symphonic Variations. Two-Piano score
  (BEVERIDGE WEBSTER) 2.50

FRENCH AND BELGIAN MASTERS
of the XVII and XVIII Centuries
Album of Selected Pieces *(PHILIPP)* 2.50
CONTENTS: BALBASTRE Romance; COUPERIN Gavotte; La Fleurie; La Bersan; Sœur Monique; DANDRIEU La Gémissante; DAQUIN Le Coucou; La Tendre Sylvie; LOEILLET Gigue; Sarabande; LULLY Air Tendre; RAMEAU L'Egyptienne; La Villageoise; SCHOBERT Allegro; VAN DEN CHEYN Fughetta.

GLAZUNOV, Alexander
Op. 72. Theme and Variations 1.75

GRANADOS, Enrique
12 Spanish Dances. Complete 3.5
Goyescas. Suite of 6 pieces. Complete 3.7
CONTENTS: 1. Los Requiebros; 2. Coloquio en la Reja; 3. El Fandango de Candil; 4. Quejas ó la Maja y el Ruiseñor; 5. El Amor y la Muerte; 6. Serenata del Espectro.
The Maiden & the Nightingale *(PHILIPP)* 1.00
Escenas Romanticas 2.00

GRETCHANINOFF, Alexander
Op. 182. 12 Little Sketches for Children 1.25
Op. 98. Children's Album. 15 Pieces 1.25

HANDEL, George Frederick
Chaconne in G major *(PHILIPP)* 1.25

HAYDN, Franz Joseph
Concerto in D maj. *(MERTKE-PHILIPP)*
  With Cadenzas by HAYDN & HENKEL 2.00
Concerto in G maj. With Cadenzas by
  ROBERT VEYRON-LACROIX 2.00
Concerto in F major. With Cadenzas by
  ROBERT VEYRON-LACROIX 2.00

d'INDY, Vincent
Op. 25. Symphony on a French Mountain Air.
  For Orchestra & Piano. Piano solo part 3.00

ITALIAN MASTERS
of the XVII and XVIII Centuries
Album of Sonatas and Pieces *(PHILIPP)* 2.50
CONTENTS: GALUPPI Sonata; GRAZIOLI Sonata; MARCELLO Toccata; PASQUINI Toccata on a Song of a Cuckoo; ROSSI Andantino; ZIPOLI Suite.

KABALEVSKY, Dmitri
Op. 13. Sonatina No. 1 in C *(PHILIPP)* 1.25
Op. 27. 22 Pieces for Children (including our former Album of 18 Pieces) 1.75
Op. 38. 24 Preludes 3.00
Op. 39. 24 Little Pieces for Children 1.25
Op. 40. Variations *(PHILIPP)* 1.25
Op. 45. Sonata No. 2 *(PHILIPP)* 2.00
Op. 46. Sonata No. 3 *(PHILIPP)* 2.00
Op. 50. Concerto No. 3
  (The Youth Concerto). 2-Piano score 3.75
Op. 59. Rondo 1.25
Op. 60. Four Rondos 1.50
Op. 61. Preludes and Fugues 2.00

KHACHATURIAN, Aram
Concerto in D flat major. 2-Piano score 3.75
Toccata *(PHILIPP)* 1.25

MAC DOWELL, Edward
Op. 51. Woodland Sketches *(PHILIPP)* 1.50
Op. 39, No. 8. Shadow Dance *(PHILIPP)* 1.00
Op. 39, No. 12. Hungarian *(PHILIPP)* 1.00

MEDTNER, Nikolai
Album of Selected Pieces 2.50
CONTENTS: 4 Fairy Tales, Etude, Idyll, Mood Picture, Novelette, Dithyramb 75

MENDELSSOHN, Felix
Op. 35. 6 Preludes & Fugues *(Scharwenka)* 2.50

MOSZKOWSKI, Moritz
Op. 72. Virtuosity Studies "Ad aspera"
  (PHILIPP) 2.50

MOZART, Wolfgang Amadeus
Six Viennese Sonatinas 1.75
Variations "Ah, vous dirai-je, maman" 1.00
Concertos for Piano and Orchestra (with 2nd Piano in score). With Cadenzas by MOZART (unless otherwise indicated)
No. 9 in E flat major (K.271) 2.50
No. 12 in A major (K.414) 2.00
No. 14 in E flat major (K.449) 2.00
No. 15 in B flat major (K.450) 2.00
No. 17 in G major (K.453) With Cadenzas by MOZART & DOHNANYI 2.00
No. 18 in B flat (K.456) *(PHILIPP)* 2.00
No. 20 in d (K.466). Cadenzas by
  BEETHOVEN, BRAHMS & REINECKE 2.50
No. 25 in C major (K.503). With Cadenza by ROBERT CASADESUS 2.50
No. 27 in B flat major (K.595) 2.50
No. 28 in D (K.382) *(Concert Rondo)* 1.50
Variations. Complete *(BRUELL)* 3.75

INTERNATIONAL MUSIC COMPANY
511 FIFTH AVENUE   Complete catalog sent free on request   **NEW YORK CITY**

No. 41-72